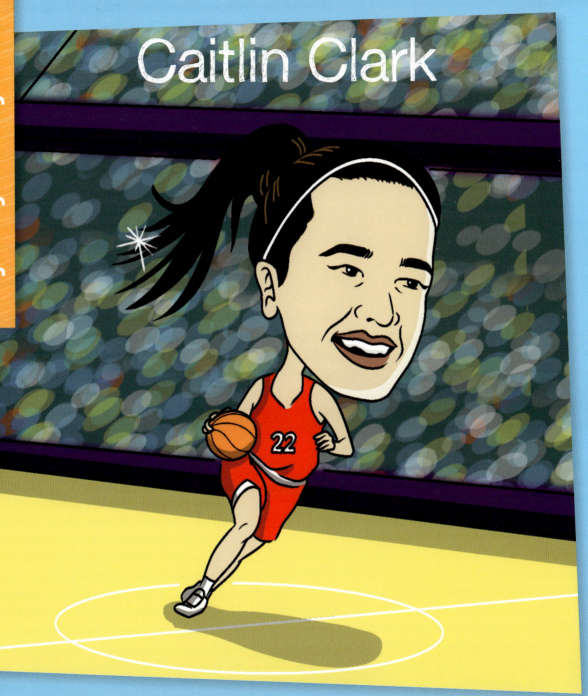

Published in the United States of America by Cherry Lake Publishing
Ann Arbor, Michigan
www.cherrylakepublishing.com

Reading Adviser: Beth Walker Gambro, MS, Ed., Reading Consultant, Yorkville, IL
Illustrator: Leo Trinidad

Photo Credits: © Jacob Boomsma/Shutterstock, 5; © Olha Didenko/Shutterstock, 7; © VicVa/Shutterstock, 9; John Mac, CC BY-SA 2.0 via Wikimedia Commons, 11, 22; John Mac, CC BY-SA 2.0 via Wikimedia Commons, 13; © ZUMA Press, Inc./Alamy Stock Photo, 15, 23; © UPI/Alamy Stock Photo, 17; © Cal Sport Media/Alamy Stock Photo, 19; © AP Photo/Jessica Hill/ASSOCIATED PRESS, 21

Copyright © 2026 by Cherry Lake Publishing
All rights reserved. No part of this book may be reproduced or utilized in any form or by any means without written permission from the publisher.

Cherry Lake Press is an imprint of Cherry Lake Publishing Group

Library of Congress Cataloging-in-Publication Data has been filed and is available at catalog.loc.gov.

Printed in the United States of America

table of contents

My Story 4

Timeline 22

Glossary 24

Index 24

About the author: When not writing, Dr. Virginia Loh-Hagan serves as the Executive Director for AANAPISI Affairs and the APIDA Center at San Diego State University. She is also the Co-Executive Director of The Asian American Education Project. She lives in San Diego with her very tall husband and very naughty dogs.

About the illustrator: Leo Trinidad is a *New York Times* bestselling comic book artist, illustrator, and animator from Costa Rica. For more than 12 years, he's been creating content for children's books and TV shows. Leo created the first animated series ever produced in Central America and founded Rocket Cartoons, one of the most successful animation studios in Latin America. He is also the 2018 winner of the Central American Graphic Novel contest.

my story

I was born in Iowa.

I was born on January 22, 2002.

I love my dog. I love baking.
I love being outside.

I also love basketball.

What do you love?

I started playing at age 5.
I played in boys' **leagues**.
I played in high school.

I was a star.

I played in college. I went to the University of Iowa.

I stayed in my home state.

I scored a lot. I broke many records. I won awards.

I was the top college scorer of all time.

I play **professional** women's basketball. I was the first **pick**.

I wear number 22.

I am popular. I have many fans. People come to my games.

Others watch my games on TV.

Do you watch sports on TV?

I love bringing joy to others.

More fans support women's basketball now.

My **legacy** lives on. I am a **force**.

I am boosting women's sports.

What would you like to ask me?

timeline

2024

1990

Born
2002

2024

2090

glossary & index

glossary

force (FORS) a person who has power

leagues (LEEGZ) groups of sports teams that play against each other

legacy (LEH-guh-see) something built over time that someone is remembered by

pick (PIK) selection or choice, such as in a professional sports draft

professional (pruh-FESH-nuhl) related to a job; describing when someone is paid for their work

index

basketball, 6, 8–21
birth, 4, 22

college, 10–13

fans, 16–18

hobbies, 6–7

Indiana Fever (team), 14–21

professional career, 14–21

talent, 8, 12, 14
televised sports, 16–17
timeline, 22–23

University of Iowa, 10–13

women's sports, 16–18